a b c d e f g

h i j k l m n

o p q r s t

u v w x y z

★ MY ★
HOOKED ON PHONICS®
DICTIONARY

Editorial Director
Dorothy M. Taguchi, Ph.D.

Vice President
Product Development and Education
Wendy Paige Bronfin

Design & Production
SunDried Penguin

Commissioned Artwork
Kathy Mitchell

Cover Illustration
Michael Arnold

Contributing Writer
Jahnna Beecham

Special thanks to Christopher Paucek and the HOP team
for their passion and dedication to children's education.

Published by
HOP, LLC
A division of Educate, Inc.
1001 Fleet Street
Baltimore, MD 21202

ISBN 1-931020-53-1

First Edition
10 9 8 7 6 5 4 3 2 1

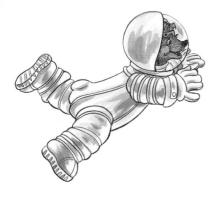

Welcome to the *My Hooked on Phonics® Dictionary*. We designed this dictionary for you and your child to enjoy together—a time for stepping into the world of words, a time for exploration and discovery. The definitions are designed to stimulate the imagination. The chalkboard pages are an invitation for your child to personalize this dictionary—to imagine, explore, practice writing letters or drawing pictures—use however your child wishes.

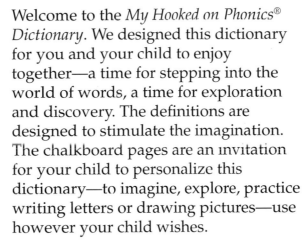

Aa

acorn

The little acorn is a seed. Watch it grow into a big oak tree.

airplane
An airplane has wings and an engine and flies high in the sky. Zoom!

alligator
See the big lizard in the swamp. An alligator's jaws can really chomp!

alphabet
The alphabet keeps the 26 letters in order ...from A to Z.

ABCDEFGHIJKLMN
OPQRSTUVWXYZ

anchor
The anchor is big and heavy. It keeps a boat from floating away.

ant

An ant has six legs, works with other ants, and can carry things that weigh more than itself.

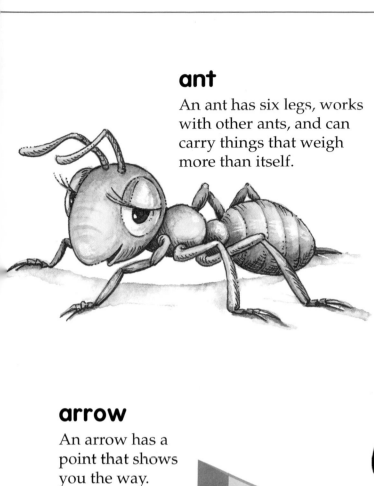

apple

An apple is a fruit that grows on a tree. It has red or green skin and is sweet and crunchy.

arrow

An arrow has a point that shows you the way.

artist

An artist creates things like paintings, photographs, or sculptures. Some artists are singers, dancers, or musicians.

astronaut

This astronaut travels in space. He's out of this world!

Bb

backpack

A backpack can hold lots of books, toys, and your lunch. You wear it on your back to keep your hands free.

balance

Pop Fox holds out his arms to keep his balance so he doesn't fall down.

bag

A bag is a container that holds different things. There are all kinds of bags, like garbage bags, grocery bags, gym bags, and paper bags.

ball

A ball is round and fun to bounce, roll, throw, kick, and catch. Throw me the ball!

balloon

A balloon is blown up when it's filled with air. If you let go of it, the balloon floats up and away.

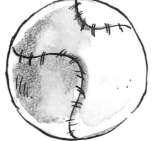

banana

A banana is a fruit that grows in a tree. Peel a banana and eat it. It's good for you, and monkeys, too.

basket

A basket has handles and can hold things like berries, flowers, or a picnic lunch.

bat

A bat is a wooden stick you swing to hit the ball when you play baseball. Home run!

bath

Mad Dog is taking a bath in the tub. Rub-a-dub-dub. This dog is clean.

bed

A bed is a cozy place where you have sweet dreams.

bee

A bee is an insect that lives in a hive. Buzz goes the bee as he makes the honey.

bell

A bell is an instrument that rings. Hear it sing. Ding dong ding!

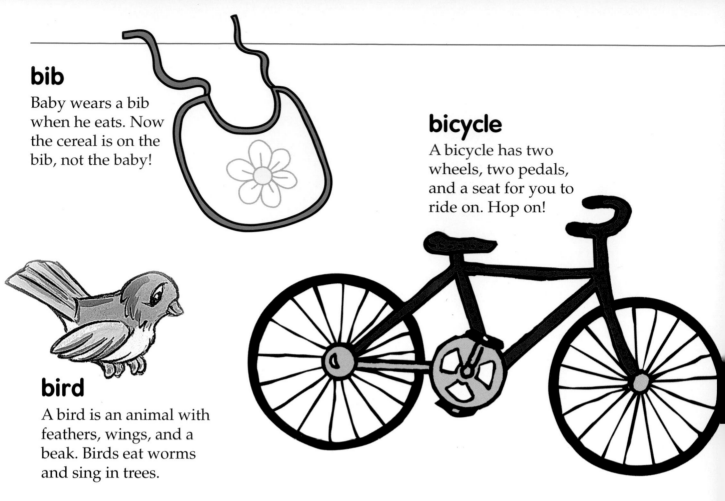

bib

Baby wears a bib when he eats. Now the cereal is on the bib, not the baby!

bicycle

A bicycle has two wheels, two pedals, and a seat for you to ride on. Hop on!

bird

A bird is an animal with feathers, wings, and a beak. Birds eat worms and sing in trees.

black

Black is the color of the sky at night. It is also the color of this crayon.

blue

The sea is the color blue. So is the sky on a clear day. Some eyes are blue.

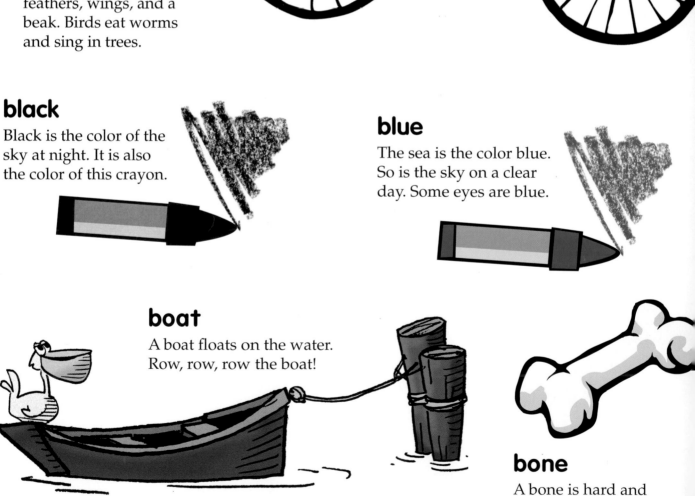

boat

A boat floats on the water. Row, row, row the boat!

bone

A bone is hard and white. Skeletons are made of them.

8

book

A book is filled with words and pictures that make up a story or give information.

bounce

When you bounce the ball, it hits the ground and then goes up again!

box

A box is handy for putting away toys and keeping your room neat.

boy

A boy is a child who will grow up to be a man.

brown

Brown is the color of tree trunks, coffee, and chocolate!

bus

A bus is like a big car that has lots of seats and carries children to school every day.

butterfly

A butterfly is an insect with beautiful wings that flutters by.

Cc

cactus

A cactus is a prickly plant that grows in the desert. It has sharp thorns, so don't touch it!

cake

A cake is a sweet baked food made with flour and eggs and other things. Kids share cake with their family and friends on their birthday!

camel

A camel is an animal with one hump or two. Camels live in the desert.

camera

Click goes the camera. You can use it to take pictures of people, places, and pets.

car

A car has 4 wheels and a motor. People drive cars to fun places and home again.

carrot

A carrot is an orange vegetable that grows in the ground. Rabbits and kids like to eat carrots. Crunch!

carry

Carry means to hold something all by yourself. You can carry books, toys, or wood—anything that's not too heavy.

castle

A castle is a big, strong fort. Kings and queens live there.

cat

A cat is an animal with four legs, whiskers, and fur. Pet it gently and hear it purr.

catch

To catch means to grab onto something when it comes your way. Pop Fox uses a net to catch bugs.

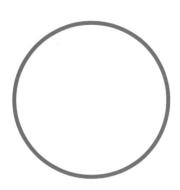

circle

A circle is a shape that is perfectly round, like a wheel.

clock

A clock lets us keep track of time for every hour of the day.

cloud

A cloud looks white and puffy and floats in the sky. Gray clouds bring rain.

cookie

A cookie is a small, sweet treat that's great for a snack.

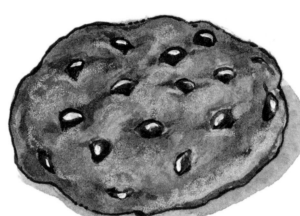

corn

Farmers grow corn in the field. Corn is a crunchy yellow vegetable that's fun to eat on the cob.

cow

A cow is an animal that lives on a farm. The milk you drink comes from a cow.

crab

A crab has a shell, eight legs, and two claws. It lives by the sea and walks sideways.

crawl

Babies can crawl before they can walk. They get around on their hands and knees.

cry

Your eyes cry big wet tears when you're sad. And sometimes you cry when you laugh really, really hard.

cup

A cup has a handle you can hold so you can drink hot chocolate.

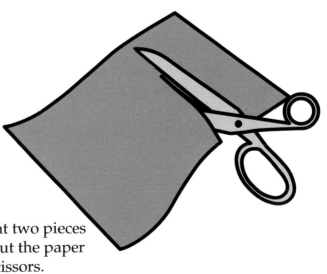

cut

When we want two pieces of paper, we cut the paper in two with scissors.

Dd

dad

Dad is another name for *father*. All dads have at least one child, while some have many children.

dictionary

A dictionary is a book that tells you what words mean. And this one shows you what they look like, too.

dig

To dig means to make a hole in the ground. We dig holes to plant flowers. Dogs dig holes to bury bones.

dime

A dime is a shiny coin worth ten pennies.

dog

A dog is an animal with four legs and fur. Dogs like to bark. Bow-wow!

doll

A doll is a toy you can play with and love.

dolphin

A dolphin lives, leaps, and plays in the ocean. Dolphins breathe through a hole in the top of their heads.

door

You use a door to go into or out of a room, house, or building. Go on in!

dragon

Dragons live in fairy tales. They are large make-believe creatures that breathe fire.

drink

A drink is something you want when you're thirsty. It can be milk, juice, or lemonade.

drum

A drum is a musical instrument you play with your hands or drumsticks. Rum-pa-um-pum!

duck

A duck is a bird that uses webbed feet to paddle around in the water. Quack quack!

Ee

eagle
An eagle is the king of birds. It has big wings and powerful claws.

ear
You have two ears, one on each side of your head. Ears help you hear music and loud rain.

Earth
We all live on a planet called Earth. The Earth is our world.

eat
When you're hungry, you eat breakfast, lunch, dinner...or a snack!

egg

Some baby animals are hatched from an egg, like birds and fish.

eight

Eight is a number. A spider has eight legs.

elephant

An elephant is a large gray animal with a long trunk, big flat ears, and saggy, baggy knees.

envelope

An envelope is a container that holds letters and things. Before you mail a letter, you put it in an envelope.

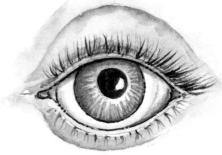

eye

You have two eyes on your face. You use your eyes to read a book, blink, and look at yourself in the mirror.

F f

fan
A fan is a machine that helps cool the air when it's hot.

feather
A feather is soft and flat and comes from a bird...and it can tickle you!

fire
A fire has flames so hot they can burn you if you get too close!

fish
A fish is an animal that lives in water. A fish uses fins to swim and gills to breathe underwater.

five
Five is a number. A hand has five fingers.

flag
A flag is a piece of fabric with colors and a design. You can wave it at a parade, a finish line, or just to see it flutter in the breeze.

flashlight

A flashlight is like a little lamp that you can carry around. When it's dark outside, you use a flashlight to help light the way.

flower

A flower is a plant that grows in the garden and smells good. Flowers have colorful petals.

foot

A foot is the part of your body at the bottom of your leg. Your feet have five toes and help you stand, run, and jump!

football

A football is a pointed ball used to play a game, also called *football*. Touchdown!

fork

A fork is a pronged tool that helps you eat food, like pancakes, peas, and pie.

four

Four is a number. A table has four legs. So does a dog.

fox

A fox is a furry animal with pointed ears, a pointed nose, and a long, bushy tail.

frog

A frog is an animal with smooth skin and webbed feet that lives in the water and on land. Ribbit! Ribbit!

Gg

garbage can
A garbage can is a big container with a tight lid that keeps the smelly trash inside.

garden
A garden is a place outside where you can grow lots of flowers or vegetables.

gas
Gas makes cars run, just like food makes you run.

giraffe
The giraffe is the tallest animal in the world. It has long legs and a very long neck.

girl
A girl is a child who will grow up to be a woman.

glasses

Glasses are two frames with glass inside that rest on your nose. Some people wear glasses to help them see clearly.

goat

A goat is an animal with four legs that climbs big rocks. Some goats have horns, and some have a beard.

grandparents

Grandparents are your parents' parents.

grapes

Grapes are small, sweet fruit that grow in a bunch on a vine. Kids eat grapes or drink grape juice.

grasshopper

A grasshopper is an insect that hops and jumps into the air!

green

Green is the color of grass, leaves, and peas.

guitar

A guitar is a stringed musical instrument. You can play songs on a guitar...and sing along!

Hh

ham

Ham is meat that comes from a pig. Some people eat ham on a sandwich.

hammer

A hammer is a tool used to hit a nail into the wall. Watch your fingers!

hand

A hand is the part of your body at the end of your arm. You use your hand to wave and say hello.

hat

A hat is a cover for your head or shade for your face. There are all kinds of hats. You can use this one to dress up like a cowboy.

heart

You have a heart inside your chest that beats and keeps you alive. It also lets you love your family...and a valentine.

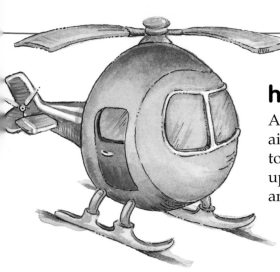

helicopter

A helicopter is an aircraft with a blade on top that lifts it straight up in the air. Up, up, and away!

helmet

Always wear a helmet to protect your head when you ride a bike, skate, or ski.

hide

You hide yourself behind or under something when you don't want anyone to see you or find you...like when you play hide-and-seek.

hippopotamus

A hippopotamus is a big gray animal that lives in rivers in Africa. It has four short legs, short ears, and a big wide mouth.

hop

To hop is like jumping—on one foot or two. Rabbits hop. So do kids when they play hopscotch.

horse

A horse is an animal with a long tail and a mane that you can saddle up and ride. A horse trots, gallops, and bucks. Whoa!

hot

In the summer the sun makes it hot outside. Then it's time for a swim!

hot dog

Take a wiener and two buns. Add ketchup and mustard. You've made a hot dog!

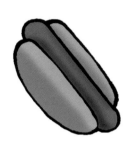

house

A house is a place where a family can live.

hug

Wrap your arms around me and squeeze. That's a big hug.

Ii

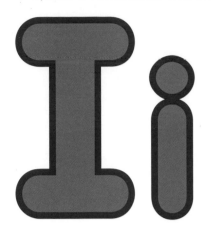

ice
When water freezes, it turns to ice. Brrrr! It's cold.

ice cream
Ice cream is a frozen, sweet treat that comes in many flavors. It tastes great in a cone or a cup.

ice skates
Ice skates are shoes or boots with a blade on the bottom that let you glide across ice.

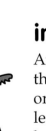

igloo
An igloo is a round house made of snow and ice.

ink
Ink is what comes out of a pen when you write. Ink can be black, red, or blue.

insect
An insect is a bug that can buzz, fly, or bite. It has six legs and some have wings.

iron
You can press a hot iron on your shirt, and the wrinkles will disappear.

island
An island is land with water all around it.

Jj

jacket
You can wear your jacket to keep you warm when it's cold outside.

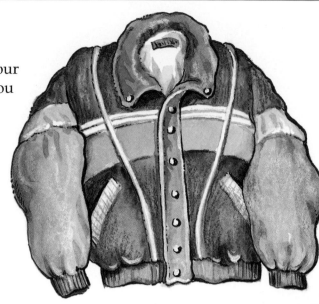

jack-in-the-box
When you wind a jack-in-the-box, a funny head pops out to surprise you.

jam
Jam is a sweet fruit spread you can put on toast.

jellyfish
A jellyfish lives and floats in the ocean like a glob of jelly. It has stringy legs, and some can sting!

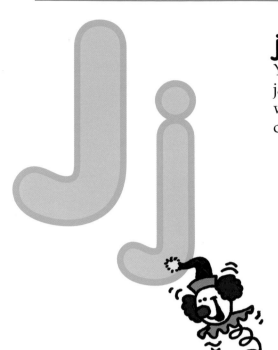

juggle
When you juggle, you try to keep lots of things in the air so they don't fall to the ground. This rat can juggle three jars in the air. That's some trick

juice

Juice is a sweet drink made from squeezing fruit.

jump

You jump when you push off the ground with your feet. You can jump into a pile of leaves. Whee!

jump rope

You can play jump rope by yourself or with two friends. They swing a rope and you jump in between!

jungle

A jungle is a thick forest where big trees, vines, birds, and monkeys live.

Kk

kangaroo

A kangaroo has short front legs, big powerful back legs, and a pouch. Kangaroos live in...and leap around...Australia.

key

A key fits in a lock. It can unlock a door, start a car, or lock up your bike.

kick

To kick a ball, swing your leg and hit it hard with your foot.

king

A king wears a crown and rules his country.

kiss

When you want to give someone a kiss, pucker up your lips and put them on his cheek! It means you care.

kitchen

The kitchen is the room in your house where all the food is cooked.

kite

You can make a kite with paper, sticks, and string. Watch it fly high in the windy sky!

knife

A knife is a tool used to cut food and things into smaller pieces. It's sharp. Be careful!

knot

A knot keeps a string or rope from coming untied. To tie one, loop and twist two ends together.

koala bear

A koala bear looks like a small bear with furry ears. Koala bears live in Australia and eat eucalyptus leaves.

Ll

ladder

A ladder can be used to reach high places. Use both hands when you climb up step by step!

ladybug

A ladybug is a small red insect with wings, sometimes with black dots.

lamb

A lamb is a baby sheep. Mary had a little lamb! Baa! Baa!

lamp

A lamp is a light that brightens a place. Some lamps are furniture that have a shade.

leaf

A leaf grows on a tree branch with lots of other leaves. Most leaves are green, but they turn red or brown when they get old.

leap

To leap is to jump high in the air. You stretch your legs to go as far as you can.

lemon

A lemon is a sour, yellow fruit. Squeeze it to make lemonade. Pucker up!

letter

A is the first letter in the alphabet, followed by **B** and **C**. The last letter is **Z**.

lettuce

Lettuce is a leafy green vegetable that makes part of a good salad.

lie

To lie down at night, take off your shoes and rest your body flat on the bed. Sweet dreams!

lion

A lion is a big cat. Male lions have big manes. The lion is the king of the jungle.

lips

A mouth has two lips. They move when you talk, and they're still when you hum.

log

A log is part of a branch or trunk of a tree that's been cut down.

love

Love is when I care for you and you care for me. You can show someone how much you love him with a hug!

Mm

mailbox
A mailbox is a container that holds letters and packages that the mailman brings.

map
A map is a picture of a place or town that shows you things like streets, bridges, rivers, and lakes.

Go to the Hut

milk
Milk is a drink that comes from a cow. It's good for building strong bones and teeth

mirror
A mirror is a special glass. When you look in it, you can see yourself.

mom
Mom is another name for *mother*. All moms have at least one child. Some have many children.

monkey

A monkey is an animal that lives in the jungle. Monkeys have long tails and hang and swing from trees.

moon

The moon is a rock that circles the earth and lights the night sky.

mop

A mop is a long-handled tool used to wash the floor.

muffin

A muffin is sweet bread baked in a small paper cup. Some kids eat muffins for breakfast.

mushroom

A mushroom is a small plant that looks a little like an umbrella.

music

Music is lots of notes put together. Music with words and instruments makes a song.

Nn

nail

A nail is a sharp piece of iron that you can hammer into two boards to hold them together.

nap

A nap is when you close your eyes and take a short rest.

necklace

A necklace is a piece of jewelry worn around your neck. It can be made of many pretty things, like beads, pearls, or a chain.

needle

A needle is a thin piece of metal used in sewing. You use it to pull thread through cloth when you sew.

nest

A nest is a bird home made of twigs and things. Baby birds are born in a nest.

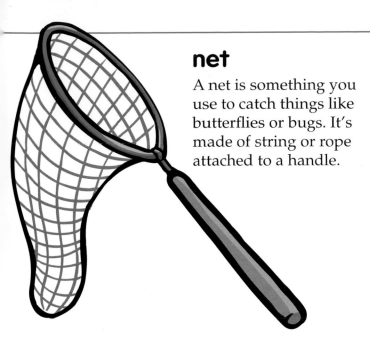

net

A net is something you use to catch things like butterflies or bugs. It's made of string or rope attached to a handle.

newspaper

A newspaper is printed every day. People read it to learn about new things happening in their town or around the world.

nickel

A nickel is a coin that's worth five pennies.

nine

Nine is a number. There are nine planets that circle our sun.

nose

A nose is in the middle of your face. You smell with it—stinky things like fish and good things like flowers.

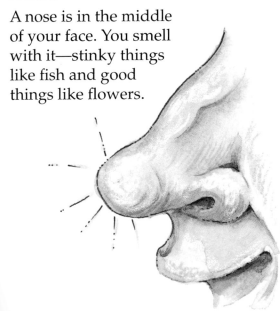

nuts

Nuts are the seeds of trees. They have hard shells and soft, chewy insides.

Oo

ocean

The ocean is filled with salt water. The oceans cover most of the earth.

octopus

The octopus is a creature that has eight arms and lives in the sea.

olive

An olive is the small green fruit from an olive tree. Press it and you get olive oil.

one

One is a number. There is only one of you.

onion

An onion is a round vegetable with lots of layers and a very strong flavor. It can make you cry when you cut it.

orange

Orange is the color of carrots and pumpkins.

orange

An orange is the name of a sweet fruit that you can peel and divide into sections to eat. Squeeze it to make orange juice.

ostrich

The ostrich is the biggest bird. It has a long neck and wings, but it can't fly.

owl

The owl is a night bird with big eyes and a hooked beak. Owls have extra bones in their necks that help them move their head around, almost in a complete circle.

ox

The ox is a big strong cow. It can pull heavy wagons.

P p

paint
Paint is liquid color. Dip a brush in it, and you can cover a wall or make a picture.

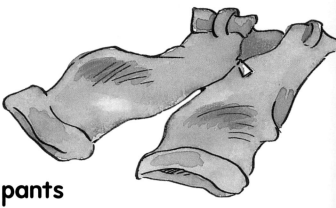

pan
A pan is a flat, metal dish with a handle. You cook with it.

pants
Pants are made from cloth. You put them on to cover your legs and keep them warm.

parrot
A parrot is a bird with bright feathers and a loud mouth. Some parrots speak human words.

peanut
A peanut grows in a shell underground. Grind a bunch of peanuts and you get peanut butter.

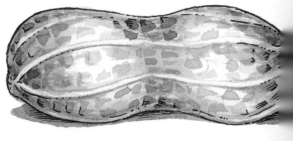

pen

A pen is a writing tool filled with ink. You can write a letter or make a drawing with it.

pencil

Use a pencil to draw or write. If you make a mistake, you can erase it.

penguin

A penguin is a black and white bird that lives at the South Pole. It uses its wings to swim, but it can't fly.

penny

A penny is a coin that is worth one cent.

pick

When you pick something, you choose from a group of things, like berries from a bush.

picnic

A picnic is a meal that you eat outside. Sometimes it comes in a basket.

pig

A pig is a farm animal with a big snout and a curly tail. Oink! Oink!

pink

Pink is the color of bubblegum and roses.

pitcher

A pitcher holds liquids like water or lemonade so you can pour them into a glass.

pizza

Pizza is a big flat pie topped with tomato sauce and cheese and anything else you want to put on it. You eat it by the slice.

planet

The earth is a planet. Nine planets circle the sun.

pocket

A pocket is a piece of material sewn on a shirt or dress. It holds things like pens or money.

pumpkin

A pumpkin is a round, orange vegetable that grows in the garden. If you can carve a face in it at Halloween, you've made a jack-o'-lantern.

purple

Purple is the color you get when you mix blue and red together.

puzzle

A puzzle is made of many strange-shaped pieces. Put them together and they make a picture.

Qq

quarter
A quarter is a coin. It is worth 25 pennies.

queen
A queen wears a crown and rules her country.

quiet
You are being quiet when you don't make a sound.

quilt
A quilt is a blanket made of pieces of material sewn together. It keeps you warm and looks pretty on a bed.

Rr

rabbit
A rabbit has strong legs, long ears, and a small tail. It's fun to watch it hop, hop, hop!

raccoon
A raccoon is an animal with rings on its tail and marks on its face that look like a mask.

rain
Rain is many drops of water that fall from clouds. It is good for growing flowers and making puddles.

rainbow
A rainbow is a big arc of colors that fills the sky after it rains.

rake
A rake is a tool we use to gather leaves on the lawn into a big pile.

rat

A rat is an animal that looks like a big mouse with a long tail.

reach

When you reach, you stretch out your hand and try to touch something.

read

To read is to see words in a book and understand the story.

red

Red is the color of stop signs and strawberries.

ribbon

A ribbon is a long, thin decoration that you can tie around a present. Bows are made of ribbon.

ring

A ring is a piece of jewelry that wraps around your finger.

robot
A robot is a machine. Some robots look and act like people.

rock
A rock is a very large stone.

roller skates
Roller skates are shoes with wheels.

rope
Rope is a strong, thick string. It can tie things together.

rug
A rug covers the floor. It is soft and feels good under bare feet.

ruler
A ruler is a straight stick that is used to measure things.

run
When you move your feet faster than a walk you run.

S s

sandwich
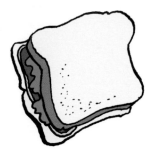
Put something good to eat between two pieces of bread, and you have a sandwich.

scissors
Scissors are a sharp tool that you use to cut paper or cloth.

7 ### seven
Seven is a number. There are seven days in a week.

shells
You can find shells at the beach. They were once the homes of sea creatures.

shirt
A shirt is a piece of clothing. You wear a shirt to keep the top half of your body warm.

shoe
A shoe protects your foot so you can walk wherever you want.

sit

When you bend your body and place your bottom on a chair, you sit.

sleep

When you're tired and close your eyes to rest your body, you sleep. Most kids like to sleep in their own bed.

slip

When you slip, you lose your balance and your feet go out from under you.

six

Six is a number. Insects have six legs.

skunk

A skunk is a black animal with a long white stripe down its back. Careful! It will make a stink if you get too close!

slide

A slide has a ladder and a long chute. Climb up the ladder and ride down to the bottom.

smile

A smile is when you feel happy and your mouth curves up on the sides.

snail

A snail is a small animal that has no bones on the inside. It carries a shell on its back.

snake

A snake has no legs, so it slithers on the ground. It has scales for skin and a long tongue that moves very quickly.

snowman

A snowman looks like a person made out of snow. Some kids add a hat, two eyes, and a carrot for a nose.

soap

Soap is something you use to wash your hands and face. It also cleans your clothes.

socks

Socks are clothing you wear on your feet. First you put on your socks and then your shoes.

spider

A spider is like an insect but has eight legs. It makes silk to spin a web.

spoon

A spoon is something you use to eat food. It has a handle and a small scoop.

square

A square is a shape that has four straight sides. Each side is the same length.

squirrel

A squirrel is an animal with a big bushy tail. It lives in trees and eats nuts.

stand

With your two feet on the ground, you can stand straight and tall.

star

A star is a shape that has five points.

strawberry

A strawberry is a sweet, red fruit. Some kids eat strawberries on cereal or all by themselves.

sun

The sun is a fiery star high in the sky that gives us light, heat, and shadows. Our planet circles the sun.

surfboard

A surfboard is a long, flat board that floats. Some people ride surfboards on waves in the ocean.

swing

A swing is a seat on a chain that you can ride back and forth. When you swing your legs, you can go higher.

T t

table
Families eat dinner at a table. A table has four legs and a flat top.

teapot
A teapot holds hot tea so you can pour it into a cup.

teeth
The teeth in your mouth are white and hard. You use them to eat and chew your food.

teddy bear
A teddy bear is a stuffed toy that feels good to hug.

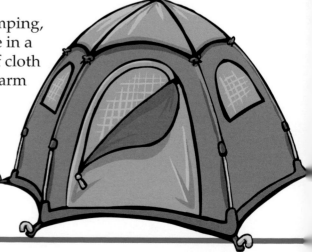

ten
Ten is a number. You have ten fingers and ten toes.

tent
When you go camping, you sleep outside in a tent. It is made of cloth and keeps you warm and dry.

three

Three is a number.
There are three
sides to a triangle.

3

tiger

A tiger is the world's
biggest cat. It has
stripes and lives in a
jungle or forest.

tongue

Your tongue is in your
mouth. It helps you eat
and talk and swallow.

toothbrush

Clean your teeth with
a toothbrush. It has
bristles and a handle.

train

A train is a string of
connected cars that
carries people and rolls
down a railroad track.

tree

A tree has a big trunk, thick branches, and lots of leaves. A tree can be fun to climb.

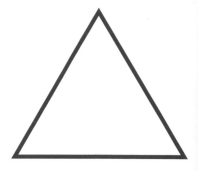

triangle

A triangle is a shape with three straight sides.

truck

A truck is a big car with a big trunk that can carry heavy loads.

turkey

The turkey is a big brown bird that can spread out its feathers like a fan. Gobble, gobble!

turtle

A turtle is an animal with a hard shell. When it's afraid, it pulls its head, legs, and tail inside.

two

Two is a number. We have two eyes, two arms, and two legs.

Uu

umbrella
An umbrella is a cover for your head with a handle. Open it so you can walk outside in the rain and stay dry.

underwear
People wear underwear under their clothes. T-shirts and underpants are two kinds of underwear.

unicorn
A unicorn is a magical white horse with one long horn on its forehead.

United States
Fifty states are joined together to form one country, the United States of America.

upside down
When you stand on your head, you're upside down.

V v

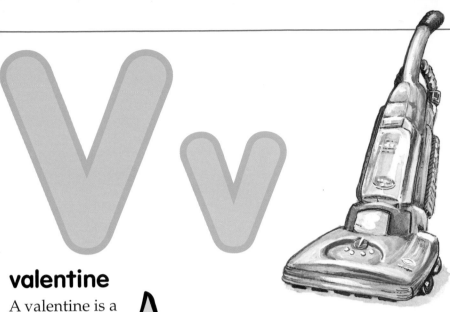

vacuum cleaner
A vacuum cleaner is a tool you use to clean. It sucks the dirt out of your rug and makes a very loud noise.

valentine
A valentine is a card that sends the message "I love you."

van
A van is a big car that is shaped like a box. It can carry your family, your dog, and you.

vase
A vase is a container. It can hold flowers and water.

vegetables
Plants like lettuce and carrots are vegetables that grow in a garden or on a farm. They are good to eat and good for you, too.

violin
A violin is a musical instrument with strings. You hold it under your chin and play it with a bow.

volcano
A volcano is a mountain with fire inside. When it gets too hot, it blows its top.

Ww

wagon
A wagon has four wheels and a handle. You can pull it.

walk
When you walk, you put one foot in front of the other.

watch
A watch is a clock you wear on your wrist.

watermelon
A watermelon is a big fruit that's green on the outside and red on the inside. It has a sweet, watery flavor and is crunchy.

wave
When you wave, you flap your hand up and down. That's how you can say hello or good-bye.

web

A spider spins a web of sticky string that helps it catch its food.

wet

When you are covered with water, you are wet.

whale

The gentle whale is the biggest animal on earth. It lives in the sea and breathes through a hole on top of its head.

whistle

A whistle is a small instrument that makes a loud tweet when you blow it.

win

When you are first in a race or a contest, you win.

window

A window is an opening in the wall of a house. You can look through it and see outside.

worm

A worm is long and thin and lives in the dirt. It has a soft body that wiggles and squirms.

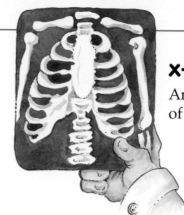

x-ray
An x-ray is a picture of your insides.

xylophone
A xylophone is a musical instrument. Tap the bars and make a song.

yak
A yak is an ox with long, shaggy hair.

yard
The ground around a house is a yard. You can play in it.

yarn
Yarn is a long string of wool or cotton. You can knit a sweater with it.

yawn

Sometimes when you're sleepy, you open your mouth really wide and take an extra deep breath. That's called a yawn.

yellow

Yellow is the color of lemons and butter.

yo-yo

A yo-yo is a round toy that rolls up and down a string.

zebra

A zebra has black and white stripes and looks like a horse.

zero

Zero is a number that means nothing. Zero is one less than one.

zipper

A zipper is something you pull to open or close your jacket or pants. It is made of metal or plastic and has teeth that fit together when closed.

zoo

A zoo is a park where animals live. It is a fun place to go with your family and friends.

Credits

Commissioned Illustrations

Kathy Mitchell—airplane, alligator, anchor, ant, butterfly, camel, camera, carrot, cookie, corn, dime, doll, eagle, Earth, ear, elephant, eye, feather, fire, flashlight, foot, fork, garden, giraffe, goat, grandparents, hammer, hand, helicopter, ice, ice cream, ice skates, iron, island, jacket, jellyfish, juice, key, king, kitchen, knife, knot, koala, lamb, lemon, lettuce, lion, love, mirror, mom, mushroom, nail, needle, nickel, nose, nut, ocean, octopus, olive, onion, orange (fruit), ostrich, peanut, pencil, penguin, penny, pocket, pumpkin, puzzle, quarter, quiet, quilt, ribbon, rung, rope, ruler, scissors, snail, snowman, soap, spider, spoon, strawberry, teddy bear, tiger, tongue, toothbrush, train, turkey, unicorn, United States, vacuum cleaner, vase, vegetables, violin, watch, web, whistle, worm, x-ray, xylophone, yak, yard, yarn, yawn, zipper, zoo

Hooked on Phonics Illustrations

The illustrations that follow were selected from our Hooked on Phonics family of programs:

acorn Doug Cushman, *Camper Kim* **apple** Lyle Booth, Hooked on Phonics alphabet **artist** ImaginEngine **astronaut** Dennis Hockerman, *Slam & Dunk Go to the Moon* **backpack** Doug Cushman, *Camper Kim* **bag** ImaginEngine **balance** Michael Arnold **ball** Doug Cushman, *Whacky Jack* **balloon** Mitchell Rose, *Pig Fun* **banana** Dennis Hockerman, *Slam & Dunk In the Dark* **basket** Ron Lipking, *Picnic at Black Rock* **bat** Doug Cushman, *Whacky Jack* **bath** Steve Haefele, *Mad Dog* **bed** Åsa Bexell, "Ned and Ted" **bee** Lyle Booth, "Alphabet Town" **bell** Lyle Booth, Hooked on Phonics alphabet **bib** ImaginEngine **bicycle** Judy Ziegler, "My Bike Ride" **bird** Dennis Hockerman, *Slam & Dunk Go to the Moon* **boat** Mitchell Rose, *Where Is Zot?* **bone** Lyle Booth, Hooked on Phonics alphabet **book** Laura Rader, "Books" **bounce** Dennis Hockerman, *Slam & Dunk and The Big Game* **box** Ron Lipking, *Picnic at Black Rock* **boy** Kathy Mitchell, *The Magic Set* **bus** Ron Lipking, *Picnic at Black Rock* **cactus** Dennis Hockerman, *Slam & Dunk Go to Hawaii* **cake** Lyle Booth, "Alphabet Town" **car** Ron Lipking, *The Race* **carry** Doug Cushman, *Camper Kim* **castle** Leslie McGuire, *A Rose, a Bridge, and a Wild Black Horse* **cat** Lyle Booth, Hooked on Phonics alphabet **catch** Michael Arnold **clock** Dennis Hockerman, *Slam & Dunk Go to the Moon* **cloud** ImaginEngine **cow** Mitchell Rose, *Detective Dog and The Lost Rabbit* **crab** Kathy Mitchell, *The Magic Set* **crawl** Michael Arnold **cry** Ron Lipking, *Picnic at Black Rock* **cup** ImaginEngine **cut** ImaginEngine **dad** Jeanne Swanson, "Look!" **dig** ImaginEngine **dog** Lyle Booth, Hooked on Phonics alphabet **dolphin** Dennis Hockerman, *Slam & Dunk Swim with Dolphins* **door** Mitchell Rose, *Detective Dog and The Lost Rabbit* **dragon** Kathy Mitchell, *The Magic Set* **drink** Steve Haefele, *Mad Dog* **drum** Laura Rader, "Crabby Couch" **duck** Mitchell Rose, *Tick-Tock* **eat** Michael Arnold **egg** Lyle Booth, Hooked on Phonics alphabet **envelope** Kathy Mitchell, *The Magic Set* **fan** ImaginEngine **fish** Dennis Hockerman, *Slam & Dunk Swim with Dolphins* **flag** Ron Lipking, *The Race* **flower** Lyle Booth, "Alphabet Town" **football** Doug Cushman, *Whacky Jack* **fox** Lyle Booth, Hooked on Phonics alphabet **frog** Doug Cushman, *Camper Kim* **garbage can** Mitchell Rose, *Where Is Zot?* **gas** Lyle Booth, Hooked on Phonics alphabet **girl** Kathy Mitchell, *The Magic Set* **glasses** Kathy Mitchell, *The Magic Set* **grapes** Judy Ziegler, "Blake the Snake" **grasshopper** Kathy Mitchell, *The Magic Set* **guitar** Lyle Booth, "Alphabet Town" **ham** ImaginEngine **hat** Lyle Booth, Hooked on Phonics alphabet **helmet** Judy Ziegler, "My Bike Ride" **hide** Steve Haefele, *Mad Dog* **hippopotamus** Mitchell Rose, *Where Is Zot?* **hop** ImaginEngine **horse** Mitchell Rose, *Mustang* **hot** ImaginEngine **hot dog** Jeanne Swanson, "Look!" **house** Mitchell Rose, *Kim Kangaroo* **hug** Doug Cushman, *Whacky Jack* **igloo** Lyle Booth, Hooked on Phonics alphabet **ink** Steve Haefele, *Mad Dog* **insect** ImaginEngine **jack-in-the-box** Kersten Brothers' Studios, "Ann's Gift" **jam** Lyle Booth, Hooked on Phonics alphabet **juggle** Lyle Booth, "Alphabet Town" **jump** Judy Ziegler, "STOMP! CRUNCH! CRACK!" **jump rope** Judy Ziegler, "The Pals" **jungle** Dennis Hockerman, *Slam & Dunk Go to Hawaii* **kangaroo** Mitchell Rose, *Kim Kangaroo* **kick** Michael Arnold **kiss** Steve Haefele, *Mad Dog in the Big City* **kite** Lyle Booth, Hooked on Phonics alphabet **ladder** Dennis Hockerman, *Slam & Dunk and The Big Game* **ladybug** Leslie McGuire, *Ann's Hat* **lamp** Dennis Hockerman, *Goblins* **leaf** Kathy Mitchell, *The Magic Set* **leap** Leslie McGuire, *Ann's Hat* **lie** Michael Arnold **lip** Steve Haefele, *Mad Dog in the Big City* **log** Lyle Booth, Hooked on Phonics alphabet **mailbox** Kathy Mitchell, *The Magic Set* **map** John Magine, *Mutt and Pup* **milk** Doug Cushman, *Whacky Jack* **monkey** Lyle Booth **moon** Esther Szegedy, *Night Is Right for Me* **mop** Lyle Booth, Hooked on Phonics alphabet **muffin** Leslie McGuire, *Ann's Big Muffin* **nap** ImaginEngine **necklace** Kathy Mitchell, *The Magic Set* **nest** Kersten Brothers' Studios, "The Hunt for the Lost Chest" **net** Lyle Booth, Hooked on Phonics alphabet **newspaper** Steve Haefele, *Mad Dog in the Big City* **owl** Dennis Hockerman, *Goblins* **ox** Lyle Booth, Hooked on Phonics alphabet **paint** Lyle Booth, Hooked on Phonics alphabet **pan** ImaginEngine **pants** Doug Cushman, *Whacky Jack* **parrot** Dennis Hockerman, *Slam & Dunk Go to Hawaii* **pen** ImaginEngine **pick** Doug Cushman, *Camper Kim* **picnic** Dennis Hockerman, *Slam & Dunk In the Dark* **pig** Lyle Booth, Hooked on Phonics alphabet **pitcher** Kathy Mitchell, *The Magic Set* **pizza** Lyle Booth **planet** Dennis Hockerman, *Slam & Dunk Go to the Moon* **queen** Lyle Booth, Hooked on Phonics alphabet **rabbit** Lyle Booth, Hooked on Phonics alphabet **raccoon** Doug Cushman, *Whacky Jack* **rain** Laura Rader, "Books" **rainbow** Lyle Booth, "Alphabet Town" **rake** Lyle Booth, "Alphabet Town" **rat** Lyle Booth, "Alphabet Town" **reach** Michael Arnold **read** Laura Rader, "Books" **robot** Judy Ziegler, "Lost and Found" **rock** Ron Lipking, *Picnic at Black Rock* **roller skates** Dennis Hockerman, *Slam & Dunk In the Dark* **rug** ImaginEngine **run** Kersten Brothers' Studios, "When the Class Bell Rings" **sandwich** Dennis Hockerman, *Slam & Dunk Go to Hawaii* **shells** Dennis Hockerman, *Slam & Dunk Swim with Dolphins* **shirt** Doug Cushman, *Whacky Jack* **shoe** Dennis Hockerman, *Slam & Dunk and The Big Game* **sit** Mitchell Rose, *Dad and Sam* **skunk** Doug Cushman, *Camper Kim* **sleep** Doug Cushman, *Camper Kim* **slide** Judy Ziegler, "My Bike Ride" **slip** Judy Ziegler, "Miss Prim's Hat" **smile** Michael Arnold **snake** Lyle Booth **socks** Lyle Booth **squirrel** Doug Cushman, *Camper Kim* **stand** Michael Arnold **sun** Lyle Booth, Hooked on Phonics alphabet **surfboard** Lyle Booth, "Alphabet Town" **swing** Kersten Brothers' Studios, "When the Class Bell Rings" **table** Ron Lipking, *Picnic at Black Rock* **teapot** Kathy Mitchell, *The Magic Set* **teeth** Steve Haefele, *Mad Dog in the Big City* **tent** Lyle Booth, Hooked on Phonics alphabet **tree** Lyle Booth, "Alphabet Town" **truck** Ron Lipking, *Tim the Truck* **turtle** Dennis Hockerman, *Slam & Dunk Swim with Dolphins* **umbrella** Lyle Booth, Hooked on Phonics alphabet **upside-down** Lyle Booth, "Alphabet Town" **underwear** Mitchell Rose, *Where Is Zot?* **valentine** Lyle Booth, Hooked on Phonics alphabet **van** Lyle Booth, Hooked on Phonics alphabet **volcano** Dennis Hockerman, *Slam & Dunk Go to Hawaii* **wagon** Lyle Booth, Hooked on Phonics alphabet **walk** Doug Cushman, *Camper Kim* **watermelon** Dennis Hockerman, *Slam & Dunk Go to the Moon* **wave** Michael Arnold **wet** ImaginEngine **whale** Dennis Hockerman, *Slam & Dunk Go to Hawaii* **win** ImaginEngine **window** Kathy Mitchell, *The Magic Set* **yo-yo** Lyle Booth, Hooked on Phonics alphabet **zebra** Lyle Booth, Hooked on Phonics alphabet

A B C D E F G

H I J K L M N

O P Q R S T

U V W X Y Z